To the sexiest, most
badass little weapon
who is also cute,
funny and caring

— STAY WINNING —

To the sexiest, most badass little weapon who is also cute, funny and caring

— STAY WHIMSY —

Printed in Dunstable, United Kingdom